M is for Masterpiece

An Art Alphabet

Written by David Domeniconi and Illustrated by Will Bullas

Sleeping Bear Press™
310 North Main Street, Suite 300
Chelsea, MI 48118
www.sleepingbearpress.com

THOMSON
★ ™
GALE

© 2006 Thomson Gale, a part of the Thomson Corporation.

Thomson, Star Logo and Sleeping Bear Press are trademarks
and Gale is a registered trademark used herein under license.

Printed and bound in China.

10 9 8 7 6 5 4 3 2 1

Library of Congress Cataloging-in-Publication Data

Domeniconi, David.
M is for masterpiece : an art alphabet / written by David Domeniconi ;
illustrated by Will Bullas.
p. cm.
Summary: "While introducing readers to famous artists, mediums, tools, and
techniques, this A-Z pictorial uses simple poetry to introduce topics such as
color, Easter Island, impressionism, Frida Kahlo, and landscape. Each letter
topic also includes detailed expository text"—Provided by publisher.
ISBN 1-58536-276-X
1. Art—Juvenile literature. I. Bullas, Will, 1949- II. Title.
N5308.D66 2006
700—dc22   2006002187

To Janet, of course. And for the girls: Veronica and Victoria,
and the new girl on the block, Gianna. And the new boy on the block, Dorian.
Special thanks to my department heads: Melanie Cardinalli, Education; Rip Matteson, Art;
Alan Spencer, English; and Dennis High, Photography. And to Will Bullas and the pros at
Sleeping Bear, Heather Hughes and Aimee Jackson; and, lest we forget, Pam Carroll.

DAVID

To Claudia who brought me Michael,
to Michael who brought us Amy,
to Michael and Amy who brought us Cassidy.

I love you.

WILL

A a

From Italy to Easter Island, from the Stone Age to the Computer Age, wherever and whenever people have lived they have made art.

Thirty thousand years ago in the caves of the Pyrenees Mountains in France, artists were at work. Drawing by lamplight, they decorated the walls and the ceilings of caves with pictures of horses and cows and bison. But these were no ordinary drawings. They were finely crafted images—images created with an artist's eye for movement, line, and shading. These animals look alive. Even now the cave drawings look modern, as if they could have been drawn by an artist living today. No one knows why these people painted these pictures, but it just might be because they are beautiful.

The *Mona Lisa* is the world's most famous painting. Why is this painting so famous? It's the smile. Ever since Leonardo da Vinci finished the painting in 1506, people have been wondering about this mysterious smile. Many books have been written about the *Mona Lisa*, but no one has figured out exactly what this young lady found so amusing.

Who was the greatest artist who ever lived? Many people would say it was Michelangelo. Michelangelo Buonarroti carved *David*, one of the world's most famous statues, and he created some of the most beautiful drawings of all time. He also painted the ceiling of the Sistine Chapel in Rome. Beginning in 1508, Michelangelo spent years painting the church ceiling. When he was finished, he had created one of the wonders of the world of art—hundreds of figures on a ceiling over 50 feet (15 meters) high portraying scene after scene from the Bible. It is perhaps the grandest work ever created by one artist.

A is for Art—
Mona Lisa, Michelangelo,
and a cow in a cave
from very long ago.

B is for Brush—
in the artist's hand,
turning paper and ink
into a magical land.

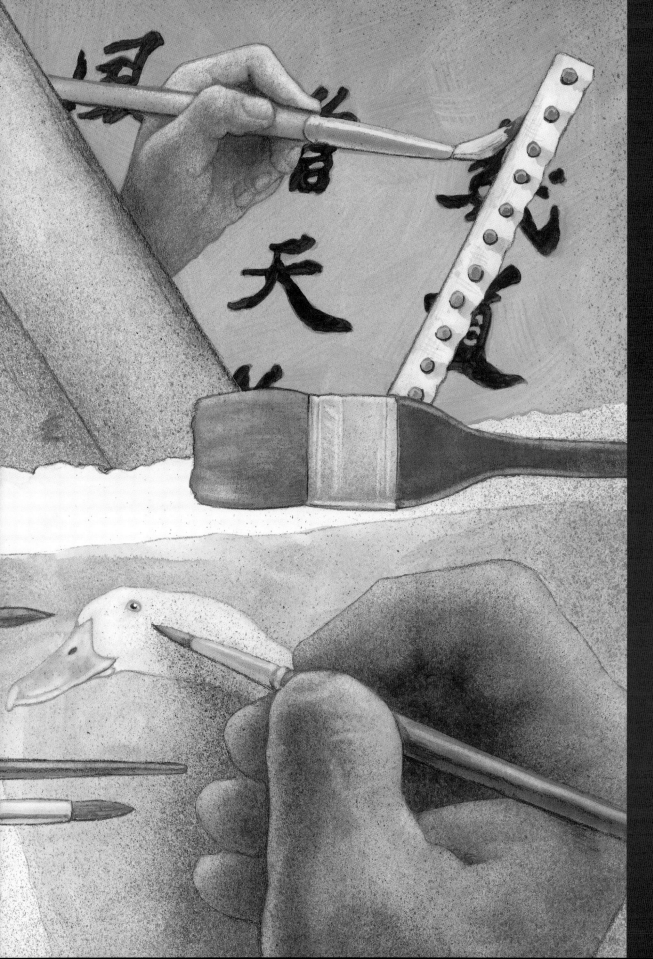

A painter uses many tools and most of them are brushes.

Brushes come in many types and sizes and shapes. Different brushes are used for different effects. In oil painting, "rounds" are used for bold stokes, "flats" for long fluid strokes, "filberts" for softening, and "fan blenders" for soft edges. In watercolor painting, "mops" cover wide areas and "riggers" dab in fine details. Oil painting brushes are usually made from hog bristle. The best watercolor brushes are sable. Asian brushes have bamboo handles and bristles of goat, wolf, or hog hair.

In China, artists have been using brush and ink for over two thousand years to create poetry and paintings. Chinese artists study many years to master the exact stroke for the perfect Chinese character or bird or leaf. During the Song Dynasty (960-1279), fantastic landscapes were painted on silk in rolls 1 foot (0.32 meters) wide and up to 30 feet (9.15 meters) long. These scrolls, called hand scrolls, were rolled up on wooden handles. Hand scrolls were meant to be unrolled a little at a time so the viewer could "walk" through the painting—down the path, over the bridge, and into the mountains.

Bb

How do artists find their way through the world of color? They use a map.

The artist's map of color is called the color wheel. The color wheel tells the artist which colors can be mixed to make another color and which colors go well next to each other. The three important points on the color wheel are yellow, red, and blue. These are the primary colors. Yellow, red, and blue stand alone. They are not made up of any other color. All the many other colors on the wheel are mixtures of yellow, red, and blue. Orange is a mix of yellow and red. Mixing blue and red makes purple. And green is only green because of a mix of yellow and blue. Colors across from each other on the color wheel are called complementary colors because they complement one another. Our eyes like to see red next to green and blue next to orange.

Artists use color in many ways. Colors can create moods and feelings. Warm colors such as yellow, red, and orange can make a painting happy. Cool colors such as blue and purple can make a painting sad. And colors can create a sense of distance. Far off mountains are often a cool blue.

In art, sometimes less is more.

The French artist Henri Matisse is best known for his use of color. Matisse believed in the power of color to reach our feelings. To get at that power he painted with only a few lines, flat shapes, and simple colors. "The simpler the color," Matisse said, "the stronger it becomes." In his most famous paintings, Matisse used only three colors: blue for the sky, green for the earth, and red for the figures.

Henri Matisse had a long career. He died in 1954 at the age of 85 and is considered a master of color and the most important French painter of the 1900s.

C is for Color.
Who even knew?
Green owed it all
to yellow and blue.

Great works of art can be created with tons of steel, or huge blocks of marble, or giant canvases and gallons of exotic colors, or a single pencil.

Drawing is the basis of most art, but drawings themselves can also be great works of art. The simplest and most versatile drawing tool is the graphite pencil. Pencils also come in a range of colors. Charcoal has been used for drawing since prehistoric times. Charcoal comes in thin sticks (called vine charcoal), charcoal pencils, or thick sticks of compressed charcoal. Other drawing tools include pastels, Conte crayons, pen and ink, and felt-tipped pens.

D is for Drawing
with pencil or pen.
And a masterpiece is made—
well, every now and then.

When we think of genius, we think of Leonardo da Vinci. Leonardo was born in Italy and lived from 1452 to 1519. He was an inventor, architect, singer, engineer, naturalist, and the painter of two of the world's most famous works of art—*Mona Lisa* and *The Last Supper*. He was also a master draftsman (a really good drawer). But Leonardo's greatest achievement may have been his notebooks. He was the first to make such great use of drawing. Over the years Leonardo filled many notebooks with detailed drawings and writings, recording his observations on the human form, nature, weapons of war, architecture, mechanics, and flying machines.

Leonardo may just have been too smart for his own good. He had so many interests and so many projects that much of what he began was never completed.

On one of the most remote islands in the South Pacific stand some of the finest examples of early art.

One thousand years ago the people of Rapanui (Easter Island) began building giant stone heads. The statues were carved of hardened volcanic ash. Some were 3 feet (0.92 meters) tall, and some were 30 feet (9 meters) tall. And some weighed as much as 90 tons (81 metric tons)—that's as heavy as 35 pick-up trucks. They hauled these stone heads as far as 7 miles (11 kilometers) and stood them up with their backs to the sea. Some believe the stone heads, the moai, are statues of ancient ancestors, but no one knows for sure. Many scientists have tried to explain how a people without modern tools could have moved these giant pieces of stone over such a distance, but no one has figured it out yet.

Ee

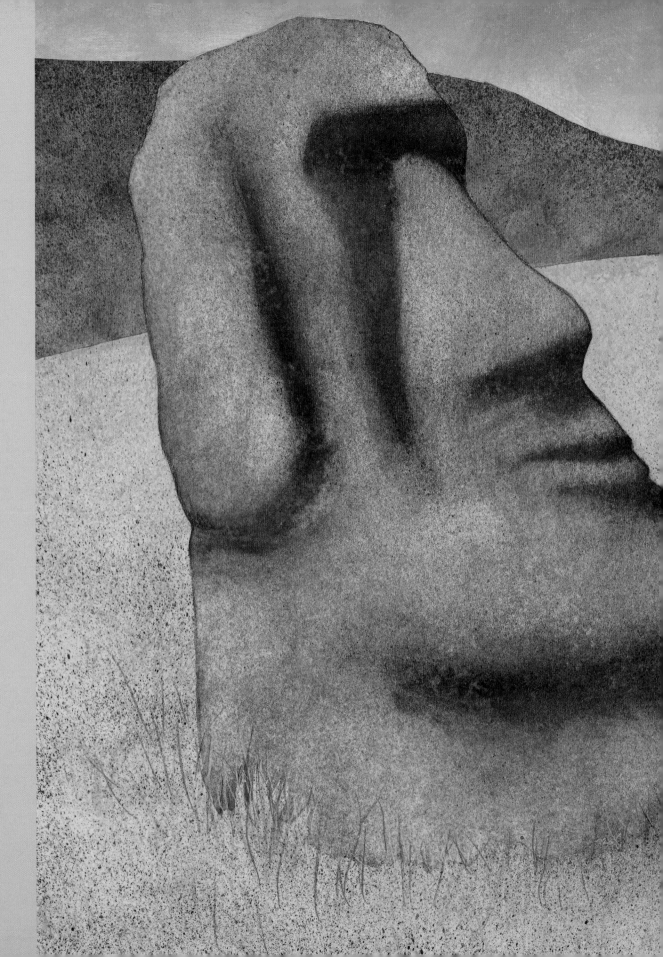

South
Pacific
Ocean

Rapa Nui

Chile

E is for Easter Island,
      statues made of stone.
How they came to be
      is a mystery still unknown.

F is for Running Fence,
    miles and miles long.
Years in the making,
    and then it was gone.

Some art just doesn't fit inside a museum, especially when it's 25 miles (40 kilometers) long.

In 1976 the artist Christo decided to build a fence. But this was no ordinary fence. Christo's fence was made of steel poles and nylon fabric and was 18 feet (5.4 meters) high and 25 miles (40 kilometers) long. *Running Fence* cut through 59 ranches in Northern California, but this fence wasn't made for animals. *Running Fence* was created for people to look at and admire and wonder what it was all about. It took almost four years and many public meetings, court hearings, and environmental reports to get approval to construct the fence across the coastal hills and right down into the ocean.

Running Fence was not built to last. After all that work, the fence was taken down after standing only 14 days.

F f

Art can take you far away from home.

One day Paul Gauguin, a stockbroker, went to an art exhibit in Paris. And he was never the same. Gauguin began buying paintings by Monet and other French artists of the day and soon he was painting. Only a few years later in 1891, he left behind his job, his family, and Paris. Gauguin turned his back on the modern world. He had become convinced he was meant to live a simpler life, away from the mad rush of the cities. Looking to get closer to nature, Gauguin moved to the island of Tahiti in the South Pacific. In Tahiti Gauguin created paintings unlike anything that had ever been seen. He found his inspiration in the bold colors and flat shapes of tribal art. One of the first artists to put his feelings in his work, Gauguin expressed his love of nature and his unhappiness with the modern world in some of the most famous paintings ever created. Eventually even Tahiti became too crowded for Gauguin and he moved on to the Marquesas Islands where he died in 1903.

Over a hundred years later, people are still fascinated by the beauty and originality of Gauguin's paintings, his life story, and the questions he asked about modern society.

G g

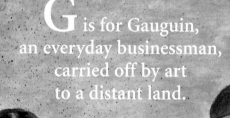

G is for Gauguin,
an everyday businessman,
carried off by art
to a distant land.

H h

H is for Horizon,
far away from here,
where objects are larger
than they might appear.

When is flat not flat?

How does an artist make a painting on a flat piece of paper look, well, not flat? They use perspective. Perspective can fool the eye into thinking something flat is deep. And what exactly is perspective? Perspective is the way things are placed in the picture. Look at this picture of a walkway lined with lampposts. How do we make the walkway look as if it leads off into the distance? The lampposts are drawn smaller and smaller as they near the horizon. The horizon is the line in the distance where the earth and the sky meet. If we draw lines connecting the tops of the lampposts, the sides of the walkway, and the tops and bottoms of the fence, all the diagonal lines in the drawing will meet at a point on the horizon. The point where all these diagonal lines meet is called the vanishing point. And then flat is not flat.

Ii

Sometimes "unfinished" art is good.

In 1874 the French government rejected a group of painters for the country's official art show in Paris. So the painters put on a show of their own, and one of the most important art movements of modern times was born. The critics hated it, but the public loved it. These artists were painting in an entirely new way. Instead of carefully copying every feature of a scene, they worked to capture the light at that exact moment. They painted outdoors and worked quickly using pure color. They didn't try to get every detail right, but rather used short brush strokes and dabs of paint to catch shapes and colors. This new art was called impressionism. The critics called the work "unfinished." But the public couldn't get enough of these colorful paintings, paintings that seemed to come to life right on the canvas. Every artist who has followed owes something to impressionism.

I is for Impressionism,
the way an artist sees
a picture of the forest,
without those pesky trees.

Claude Monet lived for the light.

Every art movement needs a founding father, or a founding mother, and Claude Monet is known as the father of impressionism. The name impressionism came from his painting in the Paris show of 1874, *Impression: Sunrise*. Monet worked outdoors on large canvases as much as 7 feet (2.1 meters) tall. But he would not paint a single leaf until the light was exactly right. Some subjects he painted over and over again, each in a different light. The last 20 years of Monet's life were spent painting in the gardens of his house in Giverny outside of Paris. Some of his most famous paintings are of his water lily pond. Monet had a long career. He painted until he was over 80 years old and produced many paintings. You will find a painting by Claude Monet in almost every major art museum around the world.

Everyone can own great works of art.

One of Japan's most famous forms of art, woodblock prints, were not made to be hung in museums or the homes of millionaires, but to be bought and enjoyed by everyone.

It takes three artists to make one woodblock print: the artist who makes the pen-and-ink drawing, the artist who carves the picture onto a woodblock, and the artist who prints the woodblock.

In Japan in the 1700s and 1800s, everyone bought books of woodblock prints. These books were full of colorful pictures of actors and landscapes, each page a work of art.

Katsushika Hokusai is the most famous of all Japanese artists. Hokusai was a master draftsman. One of the greatest artists with a brush and ink who ever lived, he made masterful drawings of Japanese landscapes and scenes from everyday Japanese life—women washing clothes, children playing games, and men fishing. Woodblock prints of his drawings were sold around the world and influenced many artists. The *Great Wave* is his most famous drawing. Hokusai had a long career and made thousands of exquisite drawings. He died at age 89 in 1849, but he was never satisfied. He believed if he could have lived to be 110, his drawings would finally have been perfect.

J is for the Japanese print
    from far across the sea.
Not the work of one artist alone,
    it takes the skills of three.

One of the artists in the West influenced by Japanese prints was Mary Cassatt. Cassatt was an American artist who lived in France. She showed her paintings alongside some of the best-known French impressionists. After viewing an exhibit of Japanese wood-block prints in Paris in the 1890s, Cassatt went on to create prints of her own, prints now considered some of the best ever made in the West. Mary Cassatt is also famous for her portraits of mothers and their children. She took great care in these drawings and paintings to get the exact pose and the perfect skin tones. Mary Cassatt's portraits of mothers and their children are some of the finest ever created.

J j

K k k

Art isn't just about pretty pictures.

When she was 18, Frida Kahlo attended medical school in Mexico City. But a streetcar accident ended her medical career. This accident left her crippled and in pain for the rest of her life. While recovering, Kahlo took up painting. Not long after, she met and married famous Mexican artist Diego Rivera. Much of Kahlo's physical pain and her stormy marriage to Rivera can be found in her paintings. She is best known for her self-portraits done in the style of Mexican folk art. Kahlo did not paint these pictures to make herself look beautiful. She painted them to tell us about herself and the world she lived in.

Since her death in 1954, Frida Kahlo's fame has grown. Today, thousands of web sites are dedicated to her. The strangeness and honesty of her work has made Frida Kahlo one of the most popular artists of all time.

K is for Frida Kahlo,
an artist and an artist's wife.
Her strange and wonderful paintings
show us a different life.

L is for Landscape—
   some hills and a tree or two.
Hang it on a wall and you have
   a room with a lovely view.

Art can move a country.

In 1859 folks living in New York City had heard of the wonders of the West, but what it actually looked like they could only imagine. That is until Albert Bierstadt returned from an expedition to the Rocky Mountains. Working from sketches and photographs he had taken on the trip, Bierstadt created a giant landscape, a 6- by 10-foot (1.8 by 3 meter) painting, *The Rocky Mountains, Lander's Peak*. New Yorkers lined up by the thousands and paid admission just to see the painting.

Despite the dangers, Bierstadt took many trips to the West. In 1863 he was one of the first Europeans to see Yosemite Valley and the first to paint it. His painting of the giant redwoods, *The Great Trees*, is 12 feet (3.7 meters) tall. Bierstadt was one of the most popular painters of his day. The wonders of his paintings inspired many folks in the East to leave home and head to the new territory, leading to the American expansion of the West.

L1

Mm

M is for Museum,
where you stand in line,
so you and famous art
can spend some quality time.

If you owned a painting worth millions of dollars, what would you do with it? Well, you just might give it away.

Fortunately for us many of the world's most famous and most valuable works of art have been donated to museums. For just the price of an admission ticket, you can spend time with the finest art ever created.

If you are going to Paris to visit the Louvre Museum, the greatest of all art museums, bring along an appreciation for fine art and some comfortable shoes. The Louvre has 8 miles (12.9 kilometers) of galleries and over a million works of art—paintings and sculpture by almost every great artist who ever lived. The Louvre is also the home of the world's most famous painting, the *Mona Lisa*. Six million people a year come to the Louvre just to get an up close look at that famous smile.

And if you are going to the Hermitage Museum in St. Petersburg, Russia, bring along those shoes and a compass. The Hermitage is the largest art museum in the world with 15 miles (24 kilometers) of galleries and three million works of art. The Hermitage has one of the largest collections of art by the European masters and many of the most famous works of Henri Matisse.

The most important and largest art museum in the United States is the Metropolitan Museum of Art in New York City. "The Met" has over two million works of art—ancient and native art, European art, and a large collection of American art. The Met is the home of Albert Bierstadt's giant painting, *The Rocky Mountains, Lander's Peak.*

Also in New York, the Museum of Modern Art contains the world's greatest collection of modern art, work created from 1880 to the present. Here you will find work by Matisse, Gauguin, Monet, Mary Cassatt, and Frida Kahlo.

Through hundreds of years and many hard times, the Navajo have kept their culture alive with the art of weaving.

The Navajo are some of the world's finest weavers. Since the 1600s in the American Southwest, grandmothers have taught mothers and mothers have taught daughters how to weave blankets "tight enough to hold water." The first blankets were made for warmth and were of simple colors: white, black, and brown. Later the weavers took bright fibers from other cloths and added color. It takes hundreds of hours to make one Navajo blanket.

Navajo weaving might have died out when wool blankets began to be made by factories, but people around the world began collecting Navajo weavings to use as rugs or hang on walls. Today fine Navajo rugs cost thousands of dollars and Navajo weavings are hung in museums around the world.

N
n

N is for the Navajo—
every mother and daughter
who kept alive the art
of a weave that will hold water.

Oo

The most famous American woman artist began life as a farm girl in Wisconsin.

But even when she was growing up on the farm, Georgia O'Keefe knew she wanted to be an artist. Right after high school, she left home to attend the Art Institute of Chicago. It wasn't long until her charcoal drawings were discovered by New York photographer Alfred Stieglitz, whom she later married. Georgia O'Keefe went on to become the most famous and successful woman artist in the country. O'Keefe's early works were of dark city skyscrapers. But her best-known paintings are inspired by nature—large paintings with up close views of colorful flowers. O'Keefe painted small flowers extra-large because she believed people never really took the time to look at a flower. Beginning in 1924 O'Keefe spent her summers in the American Southwest. There she found some of her images of desert landscapes, dried animal bones, and desert flowers. In 1946 she finally moved to New Mexico where she lived for the last 42 years of her life.

Georgia O'Keefe is remembered for being an independent, always creative, and dedicated woman artist. After almost 70 years of painting, Georgia O'Keefe died in 1986 at the age of 98. Today, you can see her work in museums around the world and at the Georgia O'Keefe Museum in Santa Fe, New Mexico.

O is for Georgia O'Keefe who painted city towers, and turned tiny petals into giant flowers.

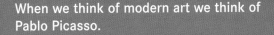

P is for Picasso,
who took things apart and then
never put all the pieces
back together again.

When we think of modern art we think of Pablo Picasso.

The son of a Spanish art instructor, Picasso was drawing at nine, painting at fourteen, and by the time he was in his thirties and living in Paris, he was one of the most famous and richest artists in the world. During his long life, Picasso worked in many, many different styles. His early work, called his blue period, was, well, blue—sad paintings of lonely, poor people. The paintings of his rose period were happier portraits of circus performers. But when Picasso experimented with images from Africa and the Pacific Islands, the art world was never the same.

Art critics hated him, the public loved him, and artists around the world followed him. Picasso experimented with the shapes he saw —images of bottles and musical instruments and even people. He didn't want to copy these images, but rather make the images fit on his canvas. So he pulled the shapes apart, flattened them out, and put them back together in unusual ways. These geometric paintings began one of the most influential art movements of modern times, cubism.

Picasso never stayed with one style long, and through his constant invention he became the most influential artist of the twentieth century. By the time of his death in 1973 at the age of 92, Picasso had created over twenty thousand drawings, paintings, and sculptures —some of the world's most valuable art.

Quillwork is the oldest form of embroidery among Native North Americans.

Long before Europeans came to this land, the people of the Great Lakes and the Plains used porcupine quills to decorate their clothes, moccasins, baskets, mats, and bags. How do you get porcupine quills? Throw a blanket over a porcupine and then pull the quills out of the blanket. Quills are sorted by size and flattened with the teeth, and then dyed with flowers, fruits, moss, or roots. The colorful quills are woven into patterns on to leather or wood. When Europeans brought glass beads to America in the 1800s, quillwork almost died out. But the art is still kept alive today by a few Native Americans. What's the secret to weaving thousands of tiny quills into a beautiful pattern—skill and patience.

Q is for Quillwork,
    from the porcupine, you see.
And how do you get those quills?
        Very carefully.

R is for Rembrandt
whose glowing light
could find a face
in the darkest night.

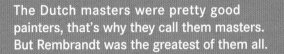

The Dutch masters were pretty good painters, that's why they call them masters. But Rembrandt was the greatest of them all.

Some of the finest artists the world has ever seen lived in Holland in the 1600s. The most famous of them is Rembrandt Harmenszoon van Rijn, the master of dark and light. Rembrandt painted many grand pictures—large, dark scenes from the Bible and group portraits of serious men. But in these night paintings a glowing light always finds the faces in the crowd. Rembrandt's faces—angry people, worried people, or people deep in thought—have never been equaled. Rembrandt began studying painting at fourteen, and when he was still in his twenties he had a large studio with many students and a big house filled with expensive art. His portraits of the wealthy citizens of Amsterdam made him wealthy. But with all his fame and fortune, Rembrandt still over spent. When he died in 1669 at the age of 63, he was penniless.

Rembrandt created so many paintings and had so many students, no one is exactly sure which paintings were done by Rembrandt and which were done by his students. Today the Rembrandt Research Project in the Netherlands uses scientific methods to find out which paintings called Rembrandt's really were painted by the master himself.

Sculpture is art that's not flat.

Rome is a city famous for sculpture, and some of Rome's finest sculptures are its marble fountains. In 1648 Gian Lorenzo Bernini created one of the most beautiful Roman fountains, *The Four Rivers Fountain*, an imaginative meeting of people, exotic creatures, and rivers from around the world.

One thousand years ago in Mexico, the Olmec people carved jade into finely detailed statues of humans and animals. These works of art are only a few inches (centimeters) tall.

In the Black Hills of South Dakota, sculpture is an entire mountain. In 1948 Korczak Ziolkowski began carving Thunderhead Mountain into a likeness of Chief Crazy Horse. Using bulldozers and explosives, Ziolkowski's family carries on today. The work will take years to complete. When the Crazy Horse Memorial is finished it will be the world's largest sculpture, almost a hundred times larger than nearby Mount Rushmore.

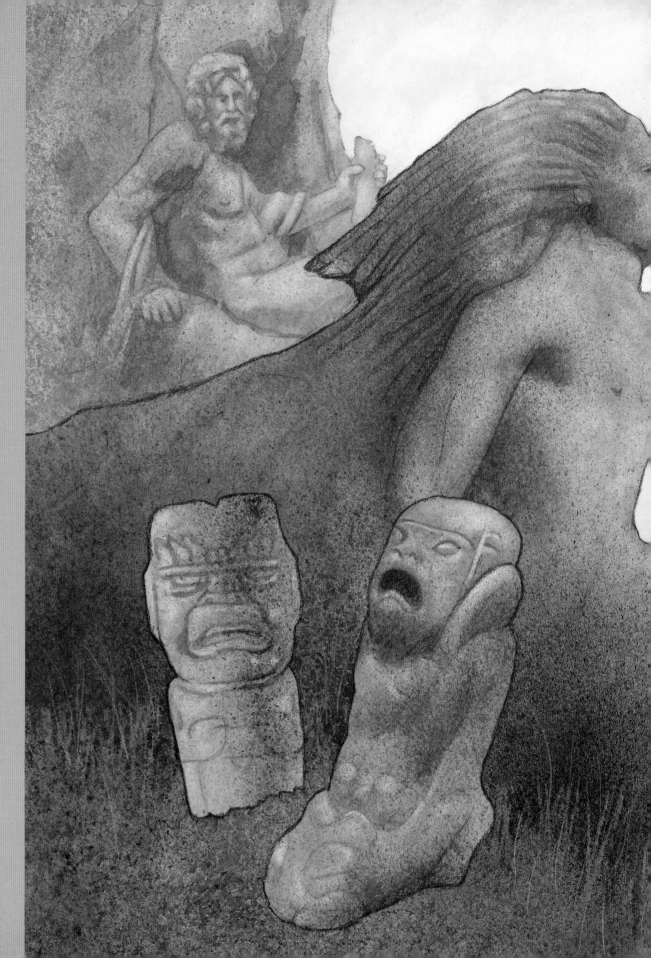

S is for Sculpture—
a fancy fountain,
one little rock,
or even Thunderhead Mountain.

When we think of sculptors, we think of Michelangelo.

Michelangelo Buonarroti was a painter, an architect, and a poet, but above all, a sculptor. Using a hammer and chisel, Michelangelo carved huge statutes from giant blocks of marble. Before beginning a new sculpture, Michelangelo would travel to the rock quarry to pick out the exact block of marble. He felt the sculpture was trapped inside the marble and all he had to do was set it free. Michelangelo's sculptures are so finely carved that hard rock comes to life as skin and cloth. His 18-foot (5.5 meter) tall statue of *David* is probably the world's most famous sculpture.

Michelangelo lived in Italy from 1475 to 1564. He was the most famous artist of his day. For much of his long life, he worked for popes and princes building grand tombs and churches that can be seen today in Florence and Rome.

What would you call the most beautiful buildings in the world? Let's call them art.

Throughout history, from the Egyptian and Mayan pyramids to Cambodian palaces to Greek and Roman temples, people have built big art called architecture. In India in 1632, Mughal Emperor Shah Jehan began building one of the finest examples of architecture the world has ever seen. It took 20 years and twenty thousand workers to complete the Taj Mahal, the final resting place for his wife, Mumtaz Mahal. Created as a vision of the Islamic paradise, the Taj Mahal is really several buildings set among gardens and pools with each tower and dome perfectly placed. The white marble of the main building is decorated with thousands of carvings and inlaid with many gems. Even though pictures of the Taj Mahal have been seen by many people, visitors cannot help but gasp when first viewing the white dome. The sight of a lifetime is a visit to the Taj Mahal under the light of a full moon.

T is for Taj Mahal
whose towering dome of white,
looks like the heavens
on a moon-filled night.

In 1889 it took Gustave Eiffel only 26 months and 250 workers to erect the tallest structure in the world. Built for the Paris Exposition, the Eiffel Tower rose up 984 feet (300 meters), taller than anything that had ever been built. At the time it was a wonder of modern engineering. The Eiffel Tower represented the hopes of the people of the 1800s in progress and science. Since its opening, the Eiffel Tower has attracted over 500 million visitors.

Sometimes the art isn't just inside the museum—sometimes the art is the museum. In 1997 in Bilbao, Spain, American architect Frank O. Gehry created a building unlike almost anything that has ever been seen. The Guggenheim Museum in Bilbao is a giant swirl of free-form metal considered one of the gems of modern architecture.

Tt

U u

U is for Untitled,
     although it does seem strange
for an artist to call art
       a name that means no name.

Sometimes the name of a painting is no name.

When a work of art is called *Untitled* it doesn't mean the artist has not given the piece a name. *Untitled* is the name.

Not all, but many "untitled" works of art, are abstract art. The beginnings of abstract art can be traced back to the early 1900s when artists began looking at art in a whole new way. They became interested not in the objects they saw, but in the shapes and colors they saw, and began experimenting with those shapes and colors. Soon artists were rearranging shapes in such unusual ways no one could even tell what they were painting. Eventually artists began making up their own shapes to create paintings and sculptures. Using their imagination, they put colors and patterns and shapes together just because they liked the way they looked. Sometimes artists will give these creative paintings names like *Green meets Yellow and Blue,* and sometimes they name them *Untitled.*

An artist will name a work of art *Untitled* for many reasons. It could be because they want the piece to speak for itself. Or it could be they want the viewer, you, to think up a title. Or could it be they just can't think of a name? You'll have to ask the artist.

"UNTITLTED"
OIL ON CANVAS
WILL BULLAS

During his short life, Vincent van Gogh was an unknown artist who lived in poverty. In 1997 his painting, *Portrait of Dr. Gachet*, sold for 90 million dollars, the highest price ever paid for a work of art.

Vincent van Gogh began life as an art dealer, teacher, and minister. Not until he was 27 in 1880 did he take up drawing and painting. From that time on van Gogh gave his life to art. Van Gogh's first paintings were dark pictures done when he lived among the poor farmers of Holland. In 1886 he moved to Paris and studied impressionism and Japanese woodblock prints. But van Gogh did not use colors like the impressionists. He picked colors that showed his inner feelings. Some of van Gogh's most famous paintings were done in Arles in the South of France where he lived and painted with Gauguin. These paintings of bright landscapes and swirling night skies were done with rugged brush strokes and bold colors.

Van Gogh suffered from mental illness and eventually took his own life when he was 37. He sold very few paintings during his life, and only after his death did van Gogh come to be regarded as one of the giants of modern art.

V v

V is for Van Gogh,
who lived by one law—
to paint what he felt,
and not what he saw.

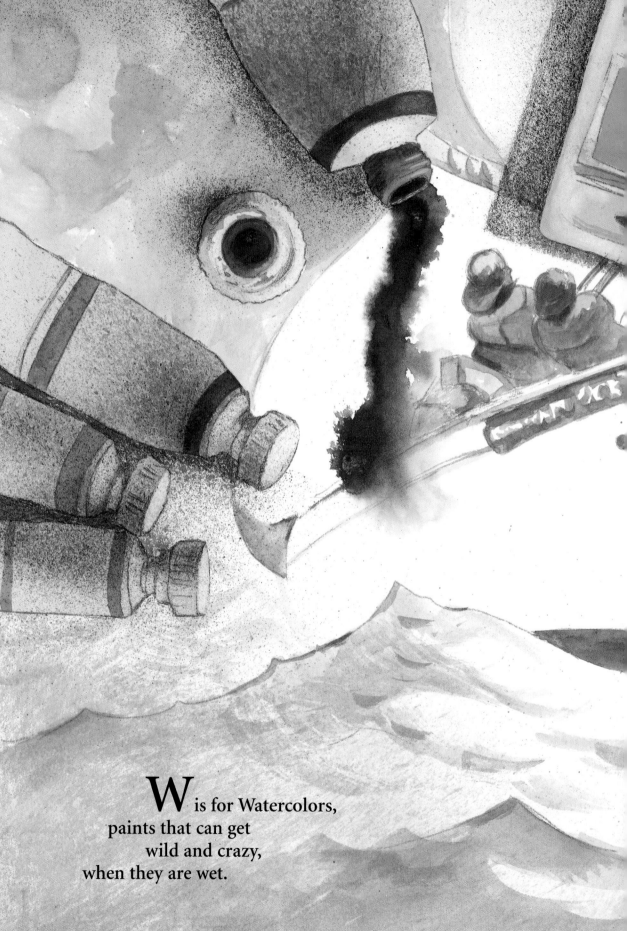

How to paint with watercolors: one, dip a brush in water; two, dab the wet brush in the paint; three, drag the brush on paper.

It sounds simple, but watercolors can have a mind of their own. What you have is water and color running loose on paper. This makes watercolors the easiest and the hardest paints to use. They are hard to use because if you are looking for an exact effect there is no going back with watercolors. Once the paint is on the paper it cannot be erased. One false stroke and a painting can be ruined. Watercolors are easy to use because an out-of-control watercolor can be a good thing. A drip, a splash, or a spill of water and color on paper can create something unexpected and beautiful. These surprises are called happy accidents.

Watercolors are also transparent, you can see through them to the paper underneath. This is what makes watercolors glow. All this—the glow, the perfect stoke, the happy accidents—is what makes watercolors special—paints that come alive on paper.

W is for Watercolors,
paints that can get
wild and crazy,
when they are wet.

Watercolors were developed in England around 1800 for painting outdoors. England has a history of famous watercolorists, but one of the masters of outdoor watercolor was an American, Winslow Homer. As a young man Homer covered the Civil War as an illustrator for *Harper's Weekly* magazine and later went on to paint large oil paintings of raging seas, some of the most famous paintings of early American art. But on his travels to England, the Caribbean, and the mountains of Upstate New York, he painted with watercolors. Down at the seaside or up in the woods, Homer would pull out his paper and watercolors, and in a matter of minutes he would create a masterpiece.

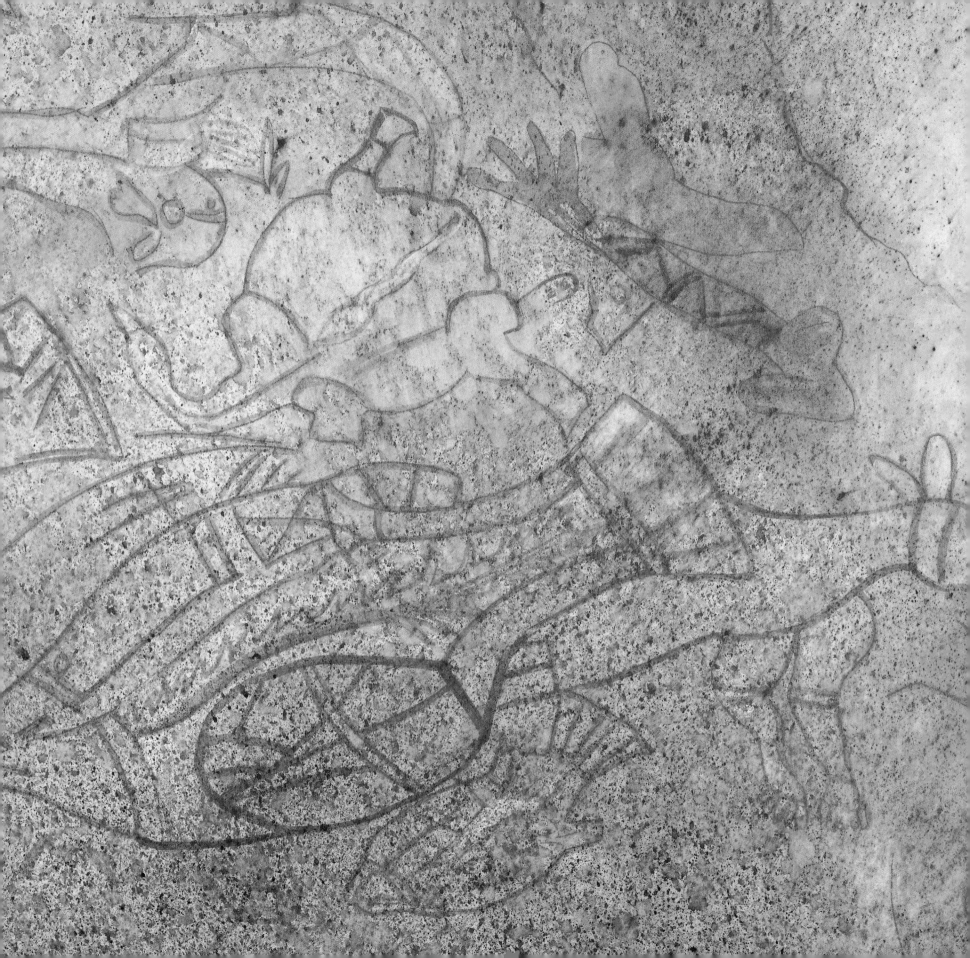

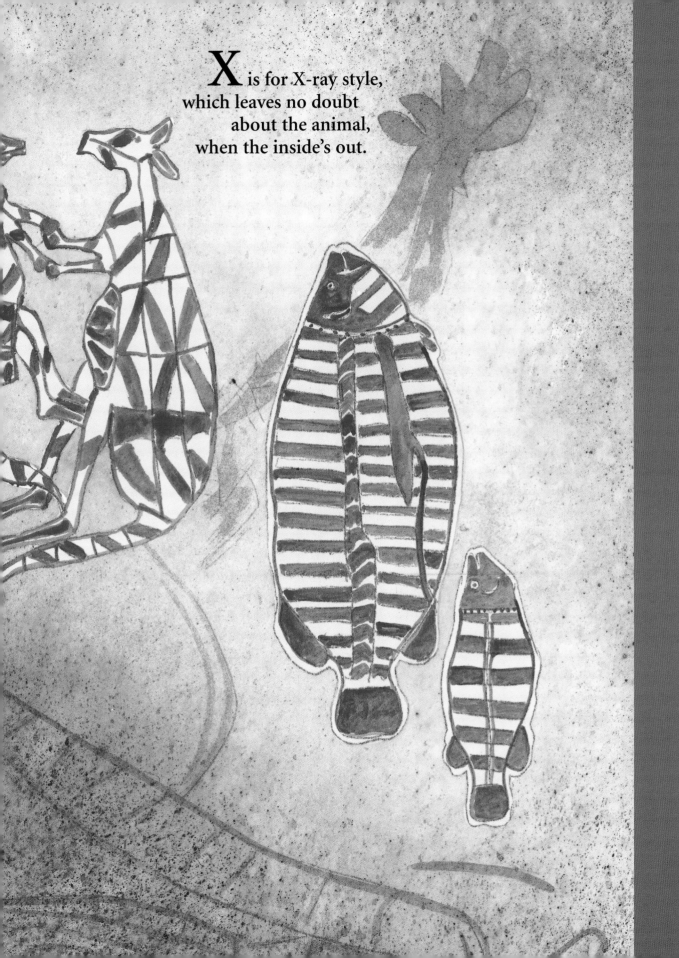

X is for X-ray style,
which leaves no doubt
about the animal,
when the inside's out.

The first people of Australia have been making art longer than anyone else in the world.

Forty thousand years ago people were creating rock art in caves of Australia. These first people of Australia lived in a mystical land. In this land they believed every rock, every creature, and every person were connected to one another. This closeness to nature can be found in their drawings of plants, animals, and people. About four thousand years ago they began drawing in x-ray style showing the bones and organs of the animals and people they drew. X-ray style is usually done with a white outline and red and yellow on the inside.

Today the ancestors of the cave artists are still making art very much like those drawings from so long ago.

X
X
X

Yy

The Yoruba have been making art on the Guinea Coast in Africa for a thousand years. Around 800 years ago, they created some of the finest bronze heads the world has ever seen. These metal sculptures were made by lost wax. Lost wax is a way of making metal sculptures from a carved piece of wax. Carved wax is covered with clay to make a mold. Then hot, liquid metal (bronze) is poured into the mold. When the metal cools what was wax is now bronze. To make the metal liquid it must be heated to 1800 degrees fahrenheit (982 degrees celsius).

The Yoruba have one of the world's oldest religions, a religion with over 400 gods. Today much of the Yoruba's sculpture is made to honor their gods. Wood and stone are carved in images of the many gods and also into figures of people and animals.

Y is for the Yoruba
who've always understood,
that art can be found
in metal and in wood.

Africa

You can hide behind art.

Like many of the people around the world,
the Yoruba make masks. Since very early
times in almost every corner of the earth,
masks have been made for theater, festivals,
ceremonies, and funerals. These works of
art are usually created by professional mask
artists. When not being worn, masks can
be kept on display, but sometimes they are
hidden. The ancient cultures of the Inca in
South America and the Egyptians made
masks of gold. On the Pacific island of New
Guinea, woven masks of spirits are 20 feet
(6 meters) tall. The native people of the
Northwest Coast of America carve beautiful
wooden masks of animals and fantastic
creatures. Japan has a long history of theater
where all the actors wear painted masks.
In Europe, carnival masks, some funny and
some scary, have been worn for hundreds
of years. But there is no place with a greater
tradition of mask making than Africa.
Everywhere in Africa people make masks—
from the animal skin masks of the Bushmen
in Southern Africa to the tall complex
wooden masks of the Yoruba.

How is it one camera takes a snapshot and another creates a work of art? Well, it all depends on who's pushing the button.

When you or I take a photograph of a mountain, we are making a recording, a recording that says what the mountain was like on the day we were there. When photographers take a picture of a mountain, they are trying to capture the spirit of the mountain. They are telling us what it feels like to be in the mountains at that time in that light. Photographers use light, texture, and movement the way a painter uses color. A zoom lens, a long lens that brings faraway things up close, is one of the photographer's tools.

Even since the first camera was invented in France in 1826, photographers have used cameras to create art.

Today fine art photographs can be found in every major art museum around the world.

Z is for Zoom,
a special camera lens.
Can a camera make art?
Well, that depends.

If you take a really good photograph—they just might name a mountain after you.

Ansel Adams first visited Yosemite when he was 14. He would come back many times. Adams spent years in Yosemite waiting for the perfect light for one perfect shot. His black-and-white photographs of Yosemite are some of the most famous pictures in photographic history. Ansel Adams dedicated his life to photography and to saving the American wilderness. His photographs of Kings Canyon helped that special place become a national park. Over his long career Adams wrote many books, and his original pictures are some of the world's most valuable photographs. When he died in 1984 at 82 years old, two hundred thousand acres in the Sierra Nevada Mountains were named the Ansel Adams Wilderness Area. And in 1985 an 11,760-foot (3,584 meter) peak near Yosemite National Park was named Mount Ansel Adams.

Zz

David Domeniconi

David Domeniconi grew up in San Francisco and graduated from San Francisco State College. He is the author of *G is for Golden: A California Alphabet* and *M is for Majestic: A National Parks Alphabet.* His illustrated travel column, "Travelog," is a regular feature in the *Santa Barbara News-Press.* He and his wife, Janet, live in the Alexander Valley near Healdsburg, California, where they own and operate an art gallery, J. Howell Fine Art.

Will Bullas

A graduate of the Brooks Institute of Fine Art in Santa Barbara, California, Will Bullas is a nationally acclaimed, award-winning artist. His original paintings are represented by several galleries throughout the U.S. He holds memberships in the Carmel Art Association, the American Watercolor Society, the National Watercolor Society, and the Knickerbocker Artists of New York. He has shown twice with the National Academy of Design at their annual shows in New York. Will has received numerous prestigious awards, and he continues to receive accolades not only for his original watercolors, but for his graphic design in packaging and poster work. Will and his wife, Claudia, live in San Francisco. You can learn more about Will at: willbullas.com.